99 THINGS

every *girl* should know

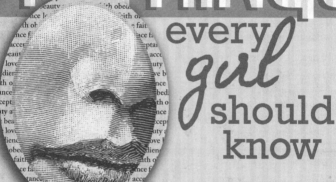

practical insights for loving God, yourself, and others

by neely mcqueen

99 Things Every Girl Should Know
Practical Insights for Loving God, Yourself, and Others
Copyright © 2010 Neely McQueen

Visit our website: simplyyouthministry.com

Credits
Author: Neely McQueen
Executive Developer: Nadim Najm
Chief Creative Officer: Joani Schultz
Editors: Lidonna Beer, Rob Cunningham, and Janis Sampson
Cover Art Director: Veronica Lucas
Designer: Veronica Lucas
Production Manager: DeAnne Lear

ISBN 978-0-7644-4955-0

10 9 8 7 6 5 4 3   17 16 15 14 13 12 11

Printed in the United States of America.

Dedication

To my small group girls (both past and present), who have allowed me into their lives.

To my daughter, who is my favorite girl in the world.

Contents

Introduction

You are beautiful, and you are of great worth!

I've made the beginning and end of this book similar, because I am convinced it is a simple truth every girl needs to know but very few really do.

A few years back I saw an article in a fashion magazine featuring women in their 30s and 40s who had written letters to their 16-year-old selves. In these letters they told themselves the things they wished they had known when they were younger, and they wrote of the heartache that it might have saved them from had they known these things. This little book is comprised of 99 things I wish I had understood when I was a teenager—things that would have helped me better understand my beauty, my worth, and my world. I've also invited some of my friends to share their stories. I find that when we hear the stories of others, we are reminded that we are not alone in this journey.

My hope for this book is that it will provide you insight and give you new confidence in who you are as a girl. As you read this book, you may find yourself with one of these possible responses:

"Nothing new here—I've heard that before." If that's your response, I would ask you to think about how that particular truth has impacted the way you live every day.

"I knew that, but I've never thought of it in that way." Ask yourself how this new understanding of that truth impacts your view of yourself and the world.

"Are you serious? I'm not sure I believe it." If you find yourself with that response, I would ask and hope that you would consider allowing it to become a good conversation starter with a friend, a parent, or a youth leader.

Don't feel like you have to read the 99 things in order. If you find yourself wanting to read about a certain topic one day and a completely different one on another day, go for it. Feel free to mark up the book and use the spaces provided to write about what you are learning.

I love being a girl, and every day I am learning more how to love the girl that I am. My prayer is that God would use this book to help you feel the same way.

Girls Rule,

Neely

Neely McQueen

BEING BFFS

1 - 5

1. The Test

Real friends don't let friends walk around school, the mall, or anywhere for that matter with stuff in their teeth, stuff hanging from their noses, or their zippers down. It might be uncomfortable to point out these "issues," but trust me, your friends will thank you! And you'll pass the real-friend test with flying colors.

STUDENT

The greatest gift of life is that we are able to share it with others. I have been blessed beyond belief with the friendships that I have. They have been my family, my support, my laughter, and a true source of happiness. I've also learned a lot of lessons about friendships throughout the years—what to do to be a good friend (and what not to do). Also, I've been learning how to deal with the fact that friends are just people and that we all make mistakes. We are always growing, always becoming, and it is a beautiful thing to do that in the company and community of others, faults and all. As more time is invested in our friendships, we become more dependent on each other. The downside of this is that we set these expectations and standards about how and when friends should be there for us and how they should act. People disappoint us, they hurt us, and they let us down. I have chosen to look at my friends and see the expectancy of our relationship. I rely on the hope of it being something long-lasting and able to endure many things. In the end, God doesn't let us down. Ever. God is the ultimate friend. I am a good friend because God has given me good friends. Having a good friendship just comes naturally when you simply enjoy one another and love the things that make you similar and different. That's what it's all about—doing life together.

—Deandra, 20

2. Friends Before Boys

At your age, to experience life and to enjoy your teenage years, friendships *must* be more important to you than having boyfriends. The truth is, boyfriends can oftentimes keep you from having a life and enjoying it. The memories from high school that still make me smile are the adventures that my friends and I had together. On the other hand, the moments that make me cringe or blush are those that I created in order to get attention from the opposite sex. Right now, it's best to live by the "friends before boys" principle.

3. It Takes One to Know One

Be the kind of friend you want to have. Are you struggling with friendships? Before you start pointing fingers at the girls around you, ask yourself, "What kind of friend am I?" and "What impact am I having on my relationships?" Being a good friend can be hard at times and require work, but the friendships that you are willing to work at will likely end up being the best friendships that you'll ever have.

Scripture:

Wounds from a sincere friend are better than many kisses from an enemy (Proverbs 27:6).

4. The Downside of Friendships

Friends can form a circle of protection from the dangers in this world. That's a good thing. On the other hand, when your circle becomes one that excludes other girls because they don't fit in, your circle has become an unhealthy clique. That's a bad thing. Cliques are dangerous when they turn girls against other girls only on the basis of petty differences. They can rob us of meeting other potential friends simply because they don't look or act the same as us. Has your circle of friendships turned ugly? Find out by asking yourself when was the last time your friends hung out with others. Or if you would lose all of your friends if one became unhappy with you? If you have a hard time answering these questions, you might want to evaluate your circle to make sure it hasn't turned into an unhealthy clique.

5. A Friend or Two

It's impossible to be best friends with everyone. Most of us work hard to have a lot of friends out of fear of being alone. A better antidote for loneliness is to simply focus on fewer friendships. Friendships that are built over time with a foundation of outrageously fun memories and truly meaningful conversations are only possible when you aren't spread thin with too many shallow friendships. I will take meaningful over shallow any day—how about you?

"Truly great friends are hard to find, difficult to leave, and impossible to forget."
— G. Randolf

Challenge

Reflect on the friendships you currently have in your life right now and the type of friend you are in those relationships. Are you fulfilled, or are your relationships lacking something?

Talk with a friend this week about your friendship. Consider taking a minute to write a thank-you note to one of your friends.

Pray for your friends. By praying for your friends, you become a better friend.

SHH...IT'S A SECRET

6 - 10

6. Three Keys to Keeping Secrets

The tricks to keeping a secret are pretty easy. First, don't tell anyone else the secret. (Wow, mind-blowing, right?) Second, don't tell anyone that you have a secret that you can't share. Third, if the secret is something that could cause harm to your friend or someone else, you are a better friend for taking the secret to a parent or another trusted adult.

7. Wisdom From Spain

Never forget this famous Spanish saying: "Si alguien te dice algo de otra persona, tambien va a hablar de ti." Translation: "Whoever gossips to you will gossip about you." I think what the Spanish are trying to tell us is that gossip is a habit—one that is hard to break and one that hurts people. Listen to the Spanish, and break the habit in your life. Here's a good rule: If you haven't said it already or if you can't say it to that person's face, don't say it to anyone else.

8. Mean Isn't Cool

Hurting other people's feelings isn't cool. Kindness always wins, even when it feels like it doesn't. I should be clear: Kindness doesn't mean that you let people walk all over you or that you lie to avoid hurting people's feelings. Kindness speaks from an attitude of gentleness and genuine concern for others regardless of what they can or can't do for you. I'll never forget Joanne, a girl I knew in high school. She was the kindest person I had ever met. Everyone wanted to be around her and be her friend. She was a few years older than me, and I remember when she was voted homecoming queen her senior year. She wasn't the prettiest or the most popular, but she was kind to *everyone*. And kindness matters to people. No one regrets being too kind, but most of us have regrets about words and actions that have hurt others. When given the option, always chose kindness.

9. Is It in Our DNA?

I've often felt as if I were born gossiping. It sometimes seems like every time I open my mouth, I speak words of gossip. It's an issue that's as old as time. We see that even the women of the Bible were challenged to guard their mouths from slander and gossip. And for whatever reason, we girls in particular struggle with our words. The good news is that God has given us the ability to overcome sin, even in those areas that feel like they are part of our DNA.

"To find out a girl's faults, praise her to her girl friends."
—Benjamin Franklin

Scripture:

A gossip goes around telling secrets, but those who are trustworthy can keep a confidence (Proverbs 11:13).

10. Sticks and Stones...

"...may break my bones, but words will never hurt me"—this is a lie, and we all know it. If I were sitting with you now, and I asked you if you had ever been hurt by gossip, I am certain that you would answer just like I would: *Yes!* Many of us have felt the pain of words spoken to us or about us. I still remember when I was in seventh grade and one of the "cool kids" made a comment about my appearance to another kid—and he said it loud enough for me to hear. While the pain is gone now, that comment hurt enough in that moment that I can still remember how I felt more than 20 years later. What I have discovered is that the people who usually hurt us are actually the ones who have been hurt. The best, and maybe the hardest, thing we can do when someone hurts us with words is to slow down for a moment and consider why that person feels the need to hurt others. If you can stop and see their pain, even for just a moment, you may be able to respond in a couple different ways. First, you might not feel so bad about what was said because you don't take it personally. You know those harsh words have little to do with you and much more to do with that person's brokenness. Second, you may be surprised to find that you are able to show compassion toward your offender. This may take a lot of practice, but I promise you that it will be worth it.

Challenge

Reflect on the times you have used your words to hurt others and the times that you have been hurt by someone else's words. Is there anyone that you need to apologize to, or is there someone that you may need to offer forgiveness?

Talk with a friend about the Spanish proverb (see page 11), and decide together if you agree or disagree with it. Commit to each other to be accountable for saying no to gossip.

Pray that God would protect your heart from the words of others and give you the discernment and strength to overcome the allure of gossip.

BOYS, BOYS & MORE BOYS

11 - 19

11. Boys Are From Somewhere Else

Maybe you have heard that girls are different from guys. And it's true that we are different:

- Our bodies (hope this isn't news to you!)

- Our perspective of the world

- Our perspective on relationships (both with guys and girls)

- Our communication (verbal and physical)

- Our perspective on the future

But in a lot of ways we are the same:

- Our desire to be understood

- Our need to be accepted

- Our ability to hope and dream

By understanding the differences, we can be better prepared as we enter into our interaction with guys. Use the wisdom of our similarities and our differences to navigate your friendships. Because of our differences, it's easy for there to be a lot of misunderstandings that can leave you feeling hurt. Try not to interpret your interactions with a guy through your perspective because it's not the same. For example, if a guy says "hi" when he walks past you, he may be just saying "hi," but sometimes what we hear is, "Hi, I think I want to marry you." (Note: This example may be overdramatized to make a point—but it also may not be overdramatized, thus making the point). All I am saying is be careful—we are different!

"On the one hand, we'll never experience childbirth. On the other hand, we can open all our own jars."
—Bruce Willis, actor

12. Making a List, Checking It Twice

Make a list of things you would like in a significant other. Make it as long or as short as you like. You never know, God might bring a guy into your life with a cute smile, a great sense of humor, and a kind heart, and who loves Jesus and enjoys long walks on the beach. When you make a list, you provide yourself guidelines for making decisions. The list can constantly change and grow as you discover more about yourself and what you think are important traits in a boyfriend. If you make the list and meet a guy who doesn't measure up, you'll be forced to reconcile the list with reality. If they can't be reconciled, you might just need to walk away.

STUDENT

When I was in eighth grade and starting to think about guys and dating, I was challenged by one of my church leaders to write out a very honest list of what I saw as my ideal future boyfriend and future husband. This list was supposed to include everything from the small inconsequential things like "has curly hair" to the deep meaningful things like "strong man of God." When I wrote that list, I was very honest with what I wanted and what I felt God had in store for me. Because of this, the list came to be a standard for any relationships and guys that came my way. I kept it in mind when I thought about dating guys, and it kept me from making some poor dating choices. In high school, when I knew myself a bit better, I decided to write the list again. It was good to refresh in my mind the standard I set for myself and improve a bit on the last list. I found it most important to write the list or work on it when I wasn't involved with a guy and wouldn't be unknowingly writing him into my list because I liked him so much. I am in college now and have kept those lists in my head as dating possibilities have come in and out of my life. I am thankful that I have been picky and stuck to the standard that God placed on my heart. It has saved me a lot of heartache and time wasted on pointless relationships and blessed me with a relationship that makes me happy and that I know makes God very happy.

– Olivia, 19

13. Love Shouldn't Hurt

Love can feel magical and bring up all sorts of emotions within that you didn't really know you could feel. Some of those feelings may even be hard to process and can lead to heartbreak or sadness. But this I do know: Love never hurts. If someone you love uses their words to make you feel less about yourself or uses their hands to hurt you, *that isn't love*. It definitely is not the kind of love that God wants for you. If right now you are in a relationship in which this is happening to you, talk to someone you trust right away.

14. Hot or Not

If you find yourself checking out the guys at school, just keep in mind that character counts a whole lot more than looks. Trust me, as I prepare myself to attend my 20-year high school reunion, I am surprised by how many guys I remember being total hotties who are now completely bald and a little round. Bald and kind is much better than bald and mean. With the right heart and character, bald can be beautiful.

15. Urban Legends

How's your relationship with your dad? Because whether you want to believe it or not, that relationship will impact how you interact with the opposite sex. The condition of that relationship—whether nonexistent or amazing—*does not necessarily have to determine* the decisions you make; however being aware of it will help you understand why you see things the way you do or why you desire certain types of relationships. The better you know yourself, the better you can readily receive God's best for you.

16. How to Keep a Guy

Guys aren't as simple as the world tries to tell us. Being physical with a guy doesn't keep his interest or earn his love. Sometimes in our minds, or in the very back of our minds, is the thought that by doing more physically we can get him to commit emotionally more to us. Not only does this not work, but it also sets up our hearts for more pain and heartbreak. It's always better to go super-slow physically even when we wish for more, rather than regret giving away a part of you that you can't get back.

17. You Complete Me

Your worth is not determined by a guy. Let me say it again: Your *worth* is not determined by a guy. Over and over, the myth that we are not complete without a man is pushed on us through romantic comedies and misguided love gurus. Sometimes it's nearly impossible for us to rise above this lie and make decisions based on truth not on our insecurities. The *only one* who completes you is Jesus. A girl who understands that truth is the kind of girl who understands her own worth. As a side note, girls who don't know their worth tend to be clinging and needy, which makes guys want to run away as fast as they can.

18. Missionary Dating

"Does it really matter if he doesn't believe the same things as I do?" I can't even begin to tell you how many times girls have asked me that question. And every time, I answer the same way. Yes, it does. When I was 16 years old, I became a Christ-follower. When I was 17, I dated a guy who wasn't one. Was it the biggest mistake I made? No. Did it affect me? Yes! Looking back I realize it was all about the little things—little things (or decisions) that kept me from amazing opportunities, which then slowed down my own spiritual growth, all to date a guy who wouldn't be in my life for longer than six months. I've seen a few women in my life enter marriages with someone who doesn't share their beliefs, and one of two things tends to happen. Either the wife eventually walks away from her faith or the marriage experiences a major strain because the husband and wife cannot agree on how to live, including how to raise their children. Both of these outcomes lead to disappointment and pain. Finding a common ground in faith is essential to a healthy and enjoyable relationship.

19. Slim Just Left Town

Statistics tell us that only a small percentage of couples who meet in junior high or high school end up as "happy marriages." Those are real slim chances. Even though we may goof around and practice writing our "future married" names using the last name of the guy(s) that we like at school, it's best to let go of the romantic "high school sweethearts" impulse. The better news is that as you get older and experience more of life in college and beyond, you'll begin to see that the world is much bigger and the chances are much better for finding happy and healthy relationships.

Challenge

Reflect this week on how you view guys and relationships. Also think about how those views affect the way you interact with guys on a daily basis.

Talk with a friend about what it means to have a healthy view of dating and guys compared to the world's views about dating and guys.

Pray for your relationships with guys and for wisdom to make not just good choices but God-honoring decisions.

LET'S TALK ABOUT SEX—AND PREGNANCY

20 - 24

20. Sex Is Complicated

Society tries to tell us that sex is easy and nothing more than a physical action. But the truth is that while sex is fun, great, and good in the context of a marriage, it is also complex and complicated, both emotionally and physically. No matter what anyone says, sex is never just casual. Don't get caught in the trap that the world is telling you about your sexuality. Sex is sacred and designed by God. God's design for sex and the exploration of our sexuality is within the context of marriage between a husband and a wife.

21. Lasting Impressions

The decisions you make now about sex will impact your life and your sex life forever. Maybe that sounds a bit dramatic, but it's the truth. Sex is one area the "what happens in Vegas, stays in Vegas" mentality just doesn't pan out. The Bible actually talks specifically about the physical consequences to sex outside of God's design and how it uniquely can have lasting effects on us, making it different than any other decision that we may make (1 Corinthians 6:12-20). Most people who have long sexual histories will tell you the same thing.

22. Just Don't Do It

Sometimes it feels like everyone is "doing it," but reality will tell you otherwise. Recent statistics have shown us that there has been a large decrease in the number of teenagers having sexual intercourse. However, statistics show us that teenagers are finding new (and unhealthy) ways to maintain their virginity while being physically intimate. If you're a girl who is trying to maintain a sense of purity and who is trying to make good choices for future relationships, just not doing *it* isn't the challenge. We're inclined to push the line to get as much as we can without breaking the rules. This means that we have made purity about following a rule. Purity and our future are not about rules but about our hopes and dreams. Don't push the line and fool around with the limits of what is and isn't sex; rather, try to understand God's heart for your purity and your future.

23. Curiosity Gone Wild

Being curious is a great character trait when it comes to education but not when it comes to our sexuality. Maybe you've heard that since you're young it's OK to "experiment" and find out what you like out there. Kiss a boy, a girl, or anyone you want—you might be surprised by what you like. But the truth is, you are still young and you are still trying to fully understand the complex way in which God created you—let alone understand love and sex. Instead of being curious about your sexuality, take this time in your life to get to know yourself. Do you have questions about your sexuality? Talk to someone you trust and who loves Jesus.

Mac [the dad]: "I thought you were the kind of girl who knew when to say when."

Juno: "I don't know what kind of girl I am."

—Juno

Becoming a teen mom was life changing; I matured abundantly, succeeded educationally, and learned what really matters. None of this came easy, however; I endured plenty of struggles along the way being a teen mom. I became pregnant at the age of 15 and had my beautiful son, Xavier, at the age of 16. I was shocked, scared, and worried. My boyfriend and I were in love, but we did not plan to have a baby. I wish someone would have told me more or provided better sex education because I am sure it would have made a difference. I also wish I would have listened much more carefully to my mother's guidance. With Xavier's arrival I was completely stripped of my freedom. My time was spent breastfeeding, diaper changing, bathing, and getting him to sleep. Maturity completely took over, although I was sleep deprived and cranky. I attended high school all through my pregnancy, and I can sincerely say it was immensely exhausting. Imagine walking around with a big belly or trying to focus in class while your baby is kicking or pushing on your diaphragm. I stayed determined, however. Even after my son, Xavier, was born, I continued my high school years—but this time it was even more difficult. I stayed up long nights doing homework after I put him to sleep and attended class bright and early each day. My hard work has paid off. I am now 19 years old and going into my sophomore year in college. I am pursing my career goal to become a registered nurse. Xavier is almost 3 years old, so now my nights are a bit easier—except, of course, when he decides to have a tantrum right before bed. I have been blessed to have an ample support system from my family. Because of their great support, I have continued my education vigorously and regained a little freedom to do things I enjoy. Being a teen mom is not glamorous. I would encourage girls to enjoy their youth and learn to love themselves. A child is a huge responsibility and should be awaited with joy.

—Jessica, 19

24. The Secret Lies of an American TV Teenager

Books, TV, and movies rarely present a real depiction of dating, sex, and teen pregnancy. Real love and life don't play out that way. Poor choices don't automatically lead to happy endings; instead, they lead to hard work and tough consequences. However, no matter the choices you have made, God has promised that he will always redeem you when you surrender to him. God's redemption includes your decisions, which he covers with grace and forgiveness when you need it most.

Challenge

Reflect on your dreams for your future and the impact your decisions about sex and purity may have on them. Reflect on God's grace in the areas where you may have slipped up, and consider how he might redeem his work in you.

Talk with a friend about how to overcome the ideas about sex that the world throws at you. Commit to honest accountability with each other.

Pray that God's grace and wisdom will fill your heart and mind when you face decisions that could impact your purity.

ALL IN THE
FAMILY

25 - 28

> **"All women become like their mothers. That is their tragedy. No man does. That's his."**
>
> —Oscar Wilde, *The Importance of Being Earnest*, 1895)

25. School's in Session

When you are with your family, you are in school. Right now you are learning how to get along with others, how to love others despite knowing everything about them, and how to have a family of your own someday. There are no formal classes or quizzes, but each day as you interact with your family, you are learning—whether you know it or not—lessons about God, relationships, marriage, and parenting. Even in the best of families there are good and bad lessons. Increase your learning by actively thinking about what you are seeing all around you—in your family and in your friends' families. Make the most of this informal education by not passively sitting back and watching it all happen, but by being an engaged student.

26. Because I Said So

I bet you hate hearing your parents say those four little words: "Because I said so." It doesn't matter what you've asked of them—as a human, your natural response is to want to push back or to rebel. Instead, why not engage in the conversation as a mature young woman by asking questions and even challenging the idea in a constructive way? Most parents don't expect their teenage kids to agree with everything they say, but good parents do expect their kids to honor their decisions. In the intensity of the discussion (or argument, if that's what it's become), be wise and reflect for a moment on the advice or decision that they're delivering and why it might be in your best interest. In the end, if you can graciously communicate that you don't agree with them but that you will honor them, you will have taken your relationship with your parents to a new level of trust and respect.

27. Broken Families

My parents' divorce shocked and devastated me. I knew my parents' marriage wasn't perfect, but I never thought it would end. And when it did, I felt lost. The one thing I thought was never going to change did—in a drastically negative way. I began to doubt a lot of things about my life. Would everything keep changing? Would anything stay the same or remain stable in my life? I began to learn that even though families aren't perfect, they are designed by God to help us grow and teach us about being a part of God's family. I found real comfort in knowing that my position in God's family was secure because God, the Father who doesn't change, has a love that is unconditional and unfailing. If your family has gone through or is going through divorce or a period of serious turmoil, reach out to people in God's family who can help restore your confidence in what a family is supposed to look like.

28. Built-In Friends

It's not always easy and sometimes feels flat-out impossible to see your siblings as friends. Instead, we often see them as built-in rivals, as those put on this earth with the sole purpose of making our lives unbearable. I'm pretty certain my older brother felt exactly that way about me. Yet in the entire world, no one else knows you or understands what life is like growing up in your family like a brother or sister does. Most people I know find out after college, when they no longer live at home, just how much they appreciate their siblings. They missed out on having an ally at home during their teenage years. Learning to see a sibling as a friend won't eliminate all the family drama, but it will probably make it a lot more fun to be in the home. Start by planning or working together on a new family tradition by the kids for the kids.

Challenge

Reflect on your family and what you have learned from them about relationships and about God.

Talk with your parents about what their families were like when they were teenagers.

Pray for your family and for the ability to enjoy and learn from them.

SEASONS OF
BEING A GIRL

29 - 30

29. Middle School Blues

When I look back over my teen years, the ones that without a doubt caused me the most pain were those unavoidable middle school years. I was half little girl and half teenager, and to add to it, I had real issues with cutting my own bangs and regretting it every time. I know that a lot of us are at our most physically awkward stage in middle school. Mix that with the fact that our peers have learned how to be as blunt and as cruel as ever, and you've got a destructive combination. Just thinking back to that time still makes my palms sweat. You can bank on this promise though: Middle School Blues don't last forever. What you feel during those years will become only a memory that is *part* of your story but not the whole of your story. Here's a great survival tip for these years: Focus on good friendships, knowing that the people who see you at your worst and don't like you any less are the ones who you'll be able to count on, not just in middle school, but for years to come. And if you happen to be one of the few girls who aren't awkward in middle school, then be kind to those less fortunate. It's a safe bet your awkward time isn't that far off.

STUDENT

Boys, boys, the problems they cause,

Breaking and entering our hearts.

Sooner or later we will have to go through menopause—

Oh, don't we just love our lady parts!

Although you and friends may fight a lot,

Things always work out in the end.

You may feel that you always get caught,

But don't fret, the problem will mend.

High school will come around soon enough;

That is where the fun will start.

The guys are finally large and buff—

Watch out, though, they also burp and fart.

In the end being a girl is great,

It was meant to be your fate.

—Bri, 16

30. High School Dreams

In high school you are in the prime of your teen years. You've become more confident in who you are, and you most likely have found a group of friends to call your own. Now is the time to start dreaming about your future. Dream about college, about an occupation, about future relationships, and about the many ways that God might use you. Now is not the time for small dreams matched by an attitude that screams, "I am just trying to get by." Rather it is the time for big dreams matched with hard work and an attitude of hope in God for your future.

Challenge

Reflect on the current season of your life. Does it fall in the category of blues or the category of dreams? Why?

Talk with a friend about your current season. If you are in middle school, talk about how you can help each other overcome the blues. If you are in high school, share your dreams for the future with each other.

Pray for perspective on your current season of life and that you will allow Jesus to be present in this time.

THE GOOD NEWS
ABOUT SCHOOL

31 - 34

31. Education Is a Gift

On mornings when your alarm clock blares too soon and you feel a little too tired and a little too cranky to go to school, remember that your education is a gift. It's a gift that not every girl in this world is given. A story in the news told us of a group of girls in Afghanistan who were finally allowed to go to school but were being attacked by people who believed girls should not be educated. On one particular day as they walked, they were attacked by men who sprayed their faces with acid. The girls were quoted as saying that they would keep going to school until they were killed because they refused to remain uneducated like the generations before them.[1] This is a powerful and painful story to keep in mind, especially on those days when your biggest challenge is getting out of bed.

32. Just Another Blonde Joke

Playing dumb is not funny or cute. There is a certain hidden pressure to not be smart or to act like you don't understand what is going on. When we play along with this pressure, it's not long before we begin to really believe it. When you buy into the deception that as a girl, you are naturally inclined to be ditzy or dumb, you'll find that the only person who gets hurt by this is you. What we learn each year in school is built on what we have learned the year before; each year prepares you for the next. In attempts to get attention by playing stupid, there's a chance you'll miss out on enough at school that it will be too hard to catch up when you need to.

---

1. www.nytimes.com/2009/01/14/world/asia/14kandahar.html

Many times in my life I have looked at education as something I just had to "get through." I slacked off in a certain class because I knew I could give minimal effort and still get the grade I wanted, and I studied just to get past my tests rather than to truly learn the material. However, my attitude toward education completely changed at the end of high school when I went on a mission trip to Nairobi, Kenya. While there, I was overwhelmed by the drive and passion with which the Kenyan children pursued their education. I was shocked to see the way those boys and girls cherished their schoolbooks as if they were treasure and worked so diligently to learn as much as they could. Even though the resources were scarce, these children maximized the little they were blessed with and pursued education with all their hearts. The experience opened my eyes to see how fortunate I am when it comes to educational opportunity, and convicted me to approach my learning according to Paul's commission in Colossians 3:23. He states, "Work willingly at whatever you do, as though you were working for the Lord rather than for people." In the past, I pursued education with only the effort needed to bring home a good report card to my parents. Now, however, I pursue education enthusiastically because I know that learning with all my heart is not about satisfying people like the verse states or making my parents proud, but rather is about fulfilling my life purpose of glorifying my Lord.

—Kristen, 20

33. Are You in the IN?

I know that right now it's hard not to feel that the most important part of school is the pressure of being popular or the pressure to fit in. I remember there were times when I was more concerned about what was going to happen between two friends than I was about completing my homework for biology. I know that a huge part of school is about friends and being social. Yet 20 years after high school I keep in contact with just *one* friend from those years in my life. No one has followed up with me about what happened between Stacey and me after our big fight or if I am still bothered that Jon didn't ask me to prom. But what I learned in high school English, history, and science still shapes how I see the world and paved the way for my future education—and it turns out that college was where I met most of my lifetime friends. Most people I know have had the same experiences when it comes to the fleeting, fading high school friendships.

34. Overachiever

If your motive is right, then trying your best is a great goal, but I know a lot of girls who work too hard to please others—like parents, teachers, or peers—to the point that they lose sight of themselves and of Jesus. If you are pushing yourself in such a way, at school or in extracurricular activities, that your body is breaking down with recurring injuries, or if you are suffering from lack of sleep or your mind is overwhelmed with worry and stress, it's time to re-evaluate who you are trying to please and how you got to this point. Consider talking with your parents about the pressure you feel to perform. Many times you'll find that the pressure isn't coming from your parents but from within yourself.

Challenge

Reflect on your attitude toward education. Are there ways you can change how you perceive school and participate in it?

Talk with a friend about how you can help each other have a better perspective on school.

Pray for those girls around the world who don't have the same freedom or rights that you do to attend school.

MIRROR, MIRROR ON THE WALL, WHAT'S THE TRUTH ABOUT BEAUTY?

35 - 40

35. What Is Beauty Anyway?

Can you define what beauty means to you? There are messages coming at us from everywhere about what makes a girl beautiful—at school, from the media, and sometimes even in our own families. I remember a time when my parents saw old family friends that we hadn't seen in a while. As we walked away, my parents made a side comment about how pretty one of the other family's daughters had become since we last saw her. It stuck out to me because I'd never heard my parents say that about another teen girl. Honestly, it threw me off for quite some time; mostly because I looked nothing like this girl, and I thought to myself that if she was the definition of pretty, then I was in trouble. This moment became a defining one for me and my definition of beauty. Sometimes I think I have two lists of what makes someone beautiful. One list is *not* real, and I know that, but for some reason I can't seem to push it out of my mind. You could say I have bought into the various messages from the world. If I told you what was on that list, you might think that I was describing a celebrity or a model who fits this unrealistic definition of beauty. But the second list consists of things I notice in people every day: having a simple, effortless look; displaying a kind heart; being a good friend; and offering a welcoming smile, to name a few. And learning to mesh these two lists into one, one that is both real and realistic, has changed my idea of what is beauty. I would challenge you to figure out for yourself what you think is beautiful and to realize that your definition doesn't have to be the same as everyone else's definition. The goal is learning to have an appreciation for external beauty while not allowing that to conceal the heart of what true beauty is.

> "There's more to life than being really, really, really good looking."
>
> —*Zoolander*

36. The Good and the Bad

I like my legs but dislike my arms. All people (supermodels included) have parts of their bodies that they don't like. Take a break today from the negative self-talk and focus on something you like about yourself. Instead of beating yourself up about all the things you think are wrong about yourself, try the opposite. You might find when you focus on the good that you are surprised by the beauty you see in yourself. When we trust God and understand that he created us, we begin to allow ourselves to see the beauty he's formed inside and outside of us. Here's a little secret too: The things I used to beat myself up over about my body turned out to be some of the things my husband likes most about me.

37. Nip/Tuck

I am sitting in my dermatologist office this morning for a little help with my adult acne (seriously?), and I am staring at a wall of brochures on "procedures" I can have done to make myself "better." And in one of those rare moments, I realize it's a lie. Procedures don't make me better—making my nose smaller or my breasts bigger won't make me a better woman. This body is just a body, or as Peter says in the Bible, a "tent" for the real me (2 Peter 1:13 NIV). My identity is not defined by what's on the outside but by *who I really am*, which comes from my heart. Changing anything and everything on the outside alters absolutely nothing on the inside.

> "Don't need your silicone, I prefer my own. What God gave me is just fine."
>
> —*Video,* India.Arie

38. The Comparison Game

Comparing yourself to others is *lame*! It hurts you, and it hurt others. The world would be a really boring place if we were all exactly the same. Stop comparing yourself to the girls around you, and you'll find that you feel better about the girl that you are. Plus, you'll have more appreciation for the unique qualities of the girls around you.

> "Calling somebody else fat won't make you any skinnier. Calling someone stupid doesn't make you any smarter."
>
> —Cady from *Mean Girls*

39. Healthy vs. Skinny

Being healthy is a good thing and a biblical thing. In 1 Corinthians 6:19, Paul calls the body a temple in which the Holy Spirit dwells. That description of our bodies brings a responsibility to take good care of them. The question or the lifelong dilemma will be to understand what "healthy" is and how to maintain it. There is an unclear line between making choices to be healthy and making choices to achieve an unrealistic image. I have been around girls who can eat whatever they want without gaining weight, but that doesn't make it right for them to put anything they want into their bodies. At the same time, I've been around girls (and this is the category I fall into) who just by smelling food begin putting on pounds, but that doesn't make it OK to not care or work toward making healthy choices. You should strive to understand your body and to make healthy choices because you understand that your body is a temple of the living Christ.

Scripture:

You say, "I am allowed to do anything"—but not everything is good for you. You say, "I am allowed to do anything"—but not everything is beneficial (1 Corinthians 10:23).

I have absolutely nothing to wear! That is a phrase that constantly reverberates off my lips three months of the year. I have always dreaded summers. I hate the way my white legs and pudgy body are suddenly exposed in the blaring sunlight. At times I've felt judgmental eyes pass over my pale arms in disgust, so year after year I sweat in misery under my blazers and cardigans, hoping autumn will come early. My struggle with body image has always been present in my life. Too often I have felt belittled and swindled by my conscience telling me that I didn't measure up to other girls. I longed to be loved, and I believed the lie that only pretty people were really loved. In order to overcome those negative thoughts, I was challenged to concentrate my focus on my passions and people. By volunteering I developed a more selfless attitude and my mind-set began to transform. I began to see my body as an active vessel that allowed me to help others, while experiencing and enjoying life. I now understand that the Creator God has given life as a gift and that I was created as a great masterpiece. However, I'm daily refined and worked on in order to achieve greatness.

—Corrie, 21

40. Crown of Creation

When I was 20 years old, I had a painful moment. I never thought I really struggled with body image until I was asked to share with others my view of myself. As I began to share what I had written down, I started to cry. I cried because I realized how much I had been fighting the lies of the world about my beauty. And I cried at the depth of how I had been impacted by God's truth regarding my beauty. In James, I read that God is "showing us off as the crown of all his creatures" (James 1:18, The Message). When I looked around the world and saw all the beauty in the world, I found it overwhelming that God viewed me as the crown—the greatest, the most beautiful—of all his creatures, and I was in awe. You see, this beauty isn't about what's in magazines or catalogs, but it's in the truth that I was *created* beautiful by the most loving and gracious God. Every day, I try to walk in that truth. It doesn't always happen, but I regularly find myself going back to that promise.

Scripture:

So, my very dear friends, don't get thrown off course. Every desirable and beneficial gift comes out of heaven. The gifts are rivers of light cascading down from the Father of Light. There is nothing deceitful in God, nothing two-faced, nothing fickle. He brought us to life using the true Word, showing us off as the crown of all his creatures (James 1:16-18 The Message).

Challenge

Reflect on your ideas of what makes a girl beautiful and how those ideas have impacted the way you see yourself.

Talk with a friend and together create a list of what makes a girl beautiful.

Pray that the truth of how God created you and how he sees you will impact your life.

THE CLOTHES
WE WEAR

41 - 42

41. Clothes and You

Our clothes tend to define who we feel that we are in the moment and how we want the world to see us. Sometimes we use clothes to get attention from guys, or sometimes we use clothes to hide in, in order to become invisible to those around us. The most important truth to know about clothes is that at the end of the day, they are just simply fabric! (Unless you're reading this in the future and clothes are made of something super-sweet, like titanium.) Our clothes don't define who we are. If we can approach clothes with that mind-set, knowing the "why" behind the clothes we choose while knowing that our motives are in the right place, we should feel free to express ourselves with our clothes. Keep in mind that, at the same time, we need to allow other girls the same freedom to express themselves without criticism.

42. Less Is More

Modesty is not only a wiser choice but can also be a more fashionable choice. Consider that when showing skin, less is more. For example, if you want to wear a sleeveless shirt, then cover up your legs; or if you want to wear a skirt, then cover up your shoulders. When showing too much skin, not only are you sending the wrong message, but you can actually take away from the style of your fashion statement.

Challenge

Reflect this week on the messages you are trying to send to others with your clothes. Do you think those messages are healthy?

Talk with a friend about your school and how groups of people have defined themselves by their clothes. Share with each other how your view of other students has been affected by their clothes, and ask if your view of them is fair.

Pray for a right perspective about appearance—that others wouldn't judge you unfairly by your appearance and that you wouldn't pass judgment on others based on theirs.

TV, MAGAZINES, AND MOVIES... OH MY!

43 - 46

43. What You See Is Not What You Get

In case you haven't heard, what you see in magazines isn't real. No one is perfect, not even Heidi Klum. I've often asked myself why we believe these images even when we know that they have been altered (thanks to hours of hair, makeup, and computer touchups). Maybe it's about *hope*. But it's a false hope that if we try hard enough we can be better; that is, we can change our looks and our current circumstances. We know it's false—we know that what we see isn't the truth. And yet we can't stop believing it and allowing it to be our standard for judging ourselves and others. If you find yourself really struggling with these images, consider taking a break from magazines for a while to allow yourself time to gain a clearer perspective.

44. Pass It On

Do we want to change what the world tells us about beauty and what it means to be "perfect"? One of the greatest ways we can say no to the lies of the media is to *stop* holding other girls to the standards we see in the media. If I know that I can't live up to those standards and if I don't want others judging me on those standards, then I need to stop judging others. When we look at other girls, let's see them for who they are—girls just like us, trying to overcome the lies from the media about beauty and perfection. We fight these messages by choosing not to pass them on to others; we free ourselves from them by freeing others from them.

45. Entertainment vs. Education

Teen-based shows, magazines, books, and movies are about entertainment; unfortunately, many of us are allowing those things to be our education. This distorted education offers flawed views on faith, relationships, beauty, families, and what it means to be a girl. We're getting superficial advice for real-life problems. Some of the teen shows targeted at you are featuring adult actors reciting lines written by adults, and most of the time those adults have agendas. There should be a big difference on how we approach our education and how we approach our entertainment. For starters, we ought to take entertainment simply at face value—it's just entertainment. And we need to ask ourselves, "Am I allowing my views to be formed by what I'm seeing, hearing, or reading here?" Have you allowed media content that's intended to be mere entertainment become more "educational" than it really ought to be?

46. Real Reality TV

Even though everything about a reality show attempts to convince you that what is happening is real, in truth there is a whole lot of make-believe happening. When you find yourself hoping and dreaming for a life like you see on reality TV, it's important to know that a producer and a storyteller often are manipulating the circumstances to catch something unreal that will draw people in to watch. They often coach the non-actors by giving them storylines that will entertain people, while they edit out most of the real-life moments. Sorry, reality TV—it's obvious that you are anything but real.

Challenge

Reflect on the different types of media that you read, listen to, or watch each week. Consider the various messages that they are trying to send about the world and about you.

Talk with a friend about how the TV shows or movies that you have watched have impacted the way you view your life.

Pray that Jesus would give the wisdom to choose wisely when selecting magazines, music, books, TV shows, and movies and that you would have the strength to follow through with the right choices.

SURVIVING THE
DIGITAL WORLD

47 - 50

47. Online Friendships

Online relationships are incomplete, lacking the substance of true relationships. It's becoming clear that the Internet is doing a pretty good job of robbing us of what it means to experience whole and authentic relationships. Sites like Facebook or MySpace are not bad, in and of themselves, until we allow them to take over how we interact with people altogether. It's easy to hide your true self online and be something that you are not, which prevents relationships from being truly authentic. Challenge yourself to process how you maintain a healthy balance between online and off-line relationships.

48. Being a (Cyber) Bully

Don't you love it when your parents say, "When I was a kid…"? I remember not being a fan of hearing those words from my mother's mouth, but that won't keep me from using them now. When I was a kid, spreading gossip was so much harder than it is nowadays. If we wanted to talk to someone about someone else, we had the following three options: Wait until we saw them at school, call them on their home phone, or write them a note to give to them as we passed them in the hall between classes. That is gossip old-school style. The Internet and texting have changed gossip. It has made it a hundred times easier to spread a rumor and to damage someone's character. That's what bullies do. Just because you aren't "saying it to their face" doesn't mean you can say whatever you want online. Being mean is being mean, no matter how it is done.

> **"When a girl ceases to blush, she has lost the most powerful charm of her beauty."**
> —Pope Gregory I

49. To Post or Not to Post

Here's an easy test for deciding whether to post a picture online: If your mom or dad wouldn't make the picture bigger, frame it, and put it up in the living room, don't post it online or send it to anyone on your phone. There are two downfalls to posting those types of pictures online. First, you are asking guys to look at you in a way that can be bad for them and that ultimately turns you into just an object. (Trust me, when a guy sees a picture of you in your two-piece swimsuit, he isn't admiring your hair or your eyes. He's thinking about things related to your swimsuit.) And second, you don't know who is looking at those pictures and what they might be doing with them. You may be thinking that you just want people to see what you did during summer break, but someone else wants to harm you by using your pictures.

STATISTIC: According to the Crimes Against Children Research Center **one in five U.S. teenagers** who regularly log on to the Internet say they **have received an unwanted sexual solicitation** via the Web. A solicitation was defined as a request to engage in a sexual activity or sexual talk or to give personal sexual information.

50. These Statistics Don't Lie

When we read statistics, we're tempted to automatically think, "That can't happen to me." In reality, however, every person who has become a victim online would likely tell you that they thought the exact same thing. There is a real danger to being online and engaging in chats with people that you don't know anything about. No matter how convinced you are that the situation is OK, do *not* agree to meet someone in person who you have met in a chat room, unless you plan on taking a parent. Trust the statistics and involve your parents in this process.

Challenge

Reflect this week on your online and text activity, and consider whether your habits online are helping or hurting your relationships.

Talk with a friend about the Internet and texting and the impact they have had on your relationships.

Pray for guidance as you make decisions about your online activity and texting and how you interact with others online.

TWEETS FROM
FRIENDS

51 - 64

51. The best trend is the one you come up with. Someone has to wear it first. It might as well be you.

52. Foul language makes any girl or woman look tacky.

53. People will make fun of you less if you can laugh at yourself.

54. Eating three meals a day is good for decision making.

55. Develop your own interests; don't change for a guy.

56. Start being now what you want to be in the future; you can change your mind later.

57. Hugs not drugs.

58. **Don't wait to think you're hot; it typically doesn't get better than it is now.**

59. **Your actions now will affect your future, and not just because your mom says so.**

60. **Elevate yourself to the standards of world-changers, not superstars.**

61. **Rules are there to guide you, not to scare you.**

62. **Don't let friends define you. Define yourself and then make friends.**

63. **Don't let it all hang out. Body parts should stay inside your clothes.**

64. **Say no to credit cards during high school and college. Those tiny pieces of plastic can ruin your life.**

HOT TOPICS

65 - 68

65. Abortion

Choosing to end a life is never easy or right. There are lots of reasons girls consider abortion, none of which will ease the pain that comes from ending a child's life. If you know someone who has chosen an abortion, now is not the time for judgment but for love and support. At the same time, if you ever find yourself in a spot where you are considering an abortion, you need to remember that abortion is not the *only* option available to you. While you cannot hide or run away from this choice, you can talk to a trusted adult, who will help you discover the many other options available to you and the unborn child.

66. Porn

Porn is bad. The end. Not only does it devalue women, but it can also destroy healthy relationships with lies about sex and sexuality. Just because we are girls (and we think it is only a guy issue) does not mean we are beyond getting hooked, so don't be tempted to just sneak a peek (by yourself or with others).

67. Cutting

I'll never forget the moment I found out about Trina's problem with cutting herself. (I've changed her name to protect my friend.) Here was a girl who on the outside seemed to everyone, including me, to have it all together. She came from a great family, went to a good school, was always surrounded with friends, and even had a serious boyfriend. In spite of those things, somewhere along the line Trina felt that she stopped being able to feel pain or joy. She never shared with me when she started cutting herself or what triggered it, but when she did begin, it was for the purpose of ensuring that she could still feel something, even if it was only physical pain. Maybe as you read about Trina, you find yourself in a similar place, where you, too, are causing physical pain to your body in order to feel alive. If that is you, then you need to know that you are not alone. There is help and there is hope for you. I want to encourage you to find an adult who you can talk to right away about what's happening in your life so that you can get the help you need.

68. Anorexia, Bulimia, and Overeating

Eating disorders are dangerous and deadly. If you've reached a point where your view of food or your body has begun to consume your thought life and decision making, then you need to know that a lot of girls have been there and have felt those same feelings. You also need to know that many of them have overcome the challenges these issues present. Wise counselors and older women who have walked this road can help you. If you or someone you know is dealing with an eating disorder, talk to a trusted adult immediately.

Challenge

Reflect throughout the week on these hot topics and how they affect your life and the lives of your friends.

Talk with a friend about each of these hot topics and where you stand on these issues.

Pray for people in your life who have dealt with these issues, and ask God to help you be a support to those who may be currently dealing with these hot topics.

THE WAR BETWEEN SHOPPING AND SAVING

69 - 71

69. We Love to Shop

I have a little issue in my life: It's called retail therapy. I love to shop, and I love to find a bargain. At times, I've used shopping to help me feel better about the things that are going wrong in my life, even though deep within I know that shopping doesn't fix the broken areas in me. I know that I am not alone in this area. In all of my life, I have only met a handful of girls who don't enjoy the mall or the thrill of finding an amazing bargain. Shopping is fun, and it's not wrong to enjoy a day at the mall. Keep your guard up, though, by making sure your shopping doesn't turn into a nasty habit that sets you up for financial disaster in the future. Here are a few signs it may be turning into a bad habit: First, you can't go to the mall without buying something. Second, when you look in your closet, you find things that still have tags on them even though you have had them for months. Third, your first thought when you feel like escaping stress or a challenging situation is how fast you can get to the mall.

70. Give It Away

Plenty of teen celebrities have shown us that having money isn't the answer to all of life's problems. If anything, they have proven to us that money can only make our lives more complicated and messy. After God, there is no force more powerful in this world than the love of money. That's why Jesus spent so much time talking about money. The love of money has the power to control us and convince us that we can be self-sufficient. If I have learned anything about money over the years, it is that I'm desperately trapped when I allow money to rule my life. There is no better way to make sure that money stays in the right place in our lives than to give it away. First, give God your tithe (read Leviticus

27:30 to understand what Scripture means by a tithe). This will allow the right perspective on money to win out in your life—that your money is not your own; it all belongs to God. Next, follow the big heart that God has given to you as a girl to support organizations or missionaries that are working in areas around the world. If you are looking for a great organization, check out Compassion International for their work with children.

71. A Penny a Day

Some of the best advice that I ever received as a girl about money came from a small group leader who encouraged me to set aside a portion of the money I was earning and to put it into savings. I didn't always succeed in following this instruction, especially when I first started working. However, over the years, I began to understand that wherever the money came from—whether chores, babysitting, or a job at the mall—after I gave my tithe (10 percent) to God, another 10 percent should be set aside for savings. This is one of those habits that doesn't necessarily feel good in the moment but feels great later when you find yourself in a bind needing the money. Hear this principle clearly: The younger you are, the easier it is to develop the habit of saving! The older you are, the harder it becomes as greater financial responsibilities start piling up. So, if you don't have a savings account yet, ask your mom or dad to take you to a nearby bank or credit union, and set up an account today! No, seriously—do it now!

Challenge

Reflect on how you spent and used your money this past week. Can you identify any healthy or unhealthy habits in your life when it comes to money?

Talk with a friend about saving money and giving it away. Share the areas that you want to work on with each other's help.

Pray that God would guard your heart from the temptation to allow money to rule your life, and ask God to give you a wise and generous heart when it comes to money.

JUST PLAIN
RANDOM...

72 - 76

72. Push Pause

Everyone is telling us to move, stay busy, and be productive. Now more than ever, I see teenage girls being pressured to do too much and burning out faster than ever. Listen to your body and your heart. Learn to rest and to slow down. You'll last a lot longer when you take time to pause, and you'll be surprised by how much more you can accomplish when you aren't feeling burned out and tired.

"Pay mind to your own life, your own health, and wholeness. A bleeding heart is of no help to anyone if it bleeds to death."
—Frederick Buechner, writer and theologian

73. Gender Wars

There is a movement in our world creating a war between the genders. It is a great thing to be a girl, and it is a great thing to be proud of being a girl. But neither of those great things requires us to hate guys or to feel that guys are evil.

74. Oh, Hormones!

Do I even need to write anything here? We have all felt how our responses to life change from week to week, each and every month. Our hormones are constantly changing, and those changes are accompanied by constant mood swings. These mood swings are normal and part of the joy of being a woman. Do they really affect how you respond to things? Yes. Do they give you a reason to be mean or spiteful? Nope. When you feel the urge to throw something or to yell at somebody or to cry at random iPhone commercials, slow down and ask yourself, "What is really triggering this response within me?" Your feelings may be justified, but your emotional response may be way out of line. So breathe and count to 10 or 100 or until you realize how you want to handle your feelings so that you won't regret it later.

75. Getting Help

I can't even tell you how many times I have been afraid to ask for help even though I knew I should have, and how many times I have spoken with girls who have felt the same in similar situations, though they also were very aware of their need for someone else's aid. So let's call out the lie that says we have to solve everything in our lives on our own or that asking for help is a sign of weakness and failure. In fact, asking for help is a sign of wisdom, strength, and humility. It's in this place that we realize that sometimes what life throws our way is bigger than us, that only with the help of others can we overcome it, and that's a good thing.

76. The Wisdom of Taylor Swift

Right now feels like the most important moment of your life. It seems like how you feel right now in this moment will be how you will feel forever. Enter Taylor Swift. She sings of being 15 and the moment when you feel like you know exactly what you want and the pain of finding out you were wrong. Let me give you permission to change your mind as you grow. These growing moments allow us to learn that life is longer than this "right now" and the immediate pleasure of "this" moment. Life is about the whole. Next time you make a decision, take a minute and think of your whole life—not just today or this year but the whole of your life and the impact of the decision. You won't be 15 (or 13 or 17) forever—even though it feels that way sometimes.

Challenge

Reflect on one of these topics, and examine how your life has been impacted by its truth.

Talk with a friend about these topics, and pick one that you can work on together during the week.

Pray for the wisdom to slow down and to know when you need to ask for help in life.

THE BEST
BOYFRIEND EVER

77 - 82

77. Jesus and You

I believe that when Jesus walked on the earth, he showed us something very powerful about God and God's view of women. Jesus reached out to women, he included them in his ministry, and he made them the heroines of many stories. He looked them in the eyes, and he believed in them. Jesus is looking down on you right now, and he sees you for who you are—your strengths and your weaknesses—and he *believes* in you. He wants to be in a personal relationship with you. If you haven't made the decision to follow him but you want to, then pause right now and say yes to Jesus. It's that simple. *Yes, Jesus, I believe in you. Yes, Jesus, I give my life to you. Yes, Jesus, I receive the new life you are offering me.* Read the next couple of pages to understand more about who Jesus is and how to grow in your relationship with him.

78. Jesus, You, and Others

God created us to need others, and he created the church as a place where we can find the meaningful relationships that we long for. If you aren't plugged in at a church somewhere, then find one. If you attend church already, but you haven't really plugged in yet, then join (or start) a small group for teenage girls. When you spend time with other girls who are pursuing a committed relationship with Jesus, you'll grow spiritually in a much richer, more authentic way.

79. Jesus, You, and a Mentor

No matter your age or where you are in your spiritual journey, finding a mentor is one of the best steps you can take to learn more about your faith and about Jesus. Here are few things to consider when looking for a mentor:

- A mentor is someone who is older and wiser than you—both in life and faith.

- A mentor for a girl should be a woman.

- A mentor should be someone who, when you look at her life, has qualities about her that you hope for in your own life.

Finding someone that you look up to, who is willing to meet with you on a regular basis, is an incredible gift to you and your faith. The kind of mentor you want in your life won't turn you down. All it takes is the courage to ask, so *go for it*!

80. Jesus, You, and the World

You are the only *you* in the world. God made you unique because you are needed uniquely in the world. Your personality, your talents, your heart—the whole of who you are was created for a reason. The world needs you to be you. Stop trying to be someone else, and embrace who you are. Listen to the voice of God in your life. God, in all of his glory and power, is calling you to be you, and in doing so, you will impact the world. Maybe even now you are sensing that God is calling you to do something that you or others doubt is possible. If that's the case, then know this truth: God has made a habit of using people who recognize that they can't do it without him. Don't let negative voices keep you from going after the things that God has called you to do. You are the only *you* this world has, and we need you!

> **"The place God calls you to is the place where your deep gladness and the world's deep hunger meet."**
>
> —Frederick Buechner, writer and theologian

81. Jesus, You, and Habits

Growing in your faith is your responsibility, even as a teenager. (You put the effort in, and God will take care of the actual growing.) You are never too young to begin developing good habits on your own for growing in your faith. Develop or find a plan for spending some time in God's Word daily. Don't beat yourself up if you can't do it every day. No one is perfect, and it's not about perfection anyway. It's about growing and learning in a way that keeps you moving closer to Jesus. If you don't currently keep a journal, consider starting; it can be really fun and helpful to record what God is doing in your life. Plus, there are some really cute journals out there, or maybe you can even make a distinctly personal one if you're the crafty type!

82. Jesus, You, and the Big Jump

Every week attempt to do something that makes your heart race and requires you to trust Jesus a little more. Nothing feels more empowering than facing a fear or a challenge and leaping into it. Your mom may not let you sign up to skydive any time soon, but you can find all kinds of physical, emotional, and spiritual challenges in your life to keep your faith alive.

Challenge

Reflect on Jesus this week and meditate on all that he has done in your life.

Talk with a friend and share your faith story. Include what you want to do next to grow in your faith and how your friend could help you with that.

Pray about your faith journey; thank Jesus for giving you the gift of forgiveness and salvation, and ask him to show you what steps you need to take next to continue growing.

OLD-SCHOOL
LADIES

83 - 89

Women are an important part of Scripture. Sometimes their stories go untold, so it's important for you to learn about them and to understand that you as a teenage girl can be part of what God is at work doing now in this time period.

83. Jael

Jael was the Laura Croft: Tomb Raider of the Bible. Jael's story can be found in Judges 4. Here is a woman who saw people being unfair to God's people and then took action with her own hands. Hers is one of the more graphic stories in the Bible—it would definitely get at least a PG-13 rating. Check this out: She took a hammer and drove a tent stake through the head of the enemy army's commander. By doing so, Jael's courage gave the Israelites the momentum to overcome their enemy. What can we learn from her? God can use women to fight with courage against oppressors who stand against him.

84. Esther

Esther wins the ultimate top model contest in the Bible. She finds herself going from rags to riches, from being an orphan to a queen. Before she knows it, she is required to depend on something other than her looks—she had to depend on her trust in God and her people. Esther changes the world and saves a generation even though the crowd may have just seen her as another pretty face. She became known on the basis of her outward appearance as a "beauty queen," but she didn't allow that label to limit the way God could use her. Don't let the way the world has labeled you keep you from the plans God has established for you.

85. Eve

I think sometimes Eve gets a bad rap. I mean, I get that she blew it when she disobeyed the one rule God had set up for her and Adam. But in all fairness to Eve, she had a conversation with a serpent, which seems pretty creepy and overwhelming to me. But her failure didn't define her. She didn't stop there or give up. She became the mother of all (wo)mankind. She is part of every person's story; that is her legacy. Eve shows us that we are not our failures—that our failures don't define who we become, no matter how big or how small the mistake.

86. Mary

Imagine you're 14 and suddenly an angel appears before you and informs you that your life is about to be *radically* changed. You are not married and you've never had sex, but you are about to become pregnant. Your world is going to be *rocked* in both good ways and bad ways. People will never see you the same, but people will never be the same because of you. That is what life was like for Mary. She was chosen as a teenage girl to be the mother of Jesus, the Savior of the world. Young and afraid, she was *chosen* by God to play one of the major roles in the greatest story ever told. Mary's response to this moment is amazing and inspiring; check it out in Luke 1:26-55. Her story confirms the truth that God wants to use everyone to change the world—girls and guys, young and old. God wants to use you to change the world. So, the question really is, will you be available like Mary?

87. The Woman at the Well

In John 4, Jesus encounters a woman at the well with a shady past. Not only does she have a questionable reputation, but she's also a Samaritan. During Jesus' time on earth, Jews and Samaritans hated each other. All this is to say, you wouldn't expect what happens to happen at the well. Jesus chooses an unlikely candidate to reveal his identity as the Messiah. Not only did he reveal this to her, but he also exposed the details of her life about her past, her sin, and her shame. In that moment the woman received a revelation of Christ, and with it she received grace and mercy. What this event demonstrates to us is that Jesus knows our deepest, darkest secrets, yet there really is nothing that can separate us from his love. The good news is that he knows not only our worst sins but our great potential as well. In verse 39 of the story, we see that many people chose to follow Jesus because of this woman and her encounter with him. Neither your story nor your sins—when surrendered to Jesus—can keep you from changing others' lives after an encounter with him.

88. The Worshiping Woman

In all four Gospels—Matthew, Mark, Luke, and John—you'll find the account of a woman who worshipped Jesus by pouring perfume on his feet and wiping them clean with her hair. This is the type of worship given when one realizes the full extent to which Jesus is worthy of worship. She knew her sin, and she knew what he would do with her sins. This forgiveness led her to one of the most passionate forms of worship in the Bible. In each account, the Gospels reveal that the people around the woman didn't understand her worship, and in some cases the people even cast judgment on her, but Jesus took her side. In one account, Jesus went so far as to say that wherever his story was heard, her story would also be told. Like this woman, we have sinned, and like her, forgiveness is freely offered to us as well. We get to choose if we will allow ourselves to go to the place where our understanding of God's grace leads us to a worship experience as passionate and as extravagant as hers.

89. The Bleeding Woman

Can you imagine having your period for 12 years straight with no end in sight and no hope for a cure? Can you imagine that because of this nonstop bleeding and the current religious laws in place, you were not considered clean and those who came in contact with you would also be unclean? Can you imagine the loneliness and hopelessness that would overcome your life? That was the life of the unnamed woman of Mark 5 until she heard about Jesus. We don't know how she found out about Jesus or how she knew he would be in her town, but once she did, she came up with a plan—a plan built on faith. Her faith was so intense and so strong that she believed if she could touch Jesus' robe, she would be healed. The cool part of the story is that she was healed instantly after touching his robe. Not only did Jesus know immediately that something miraculous had happened, but the woman knew, too. Jesus stopped everything that was happening to speak to the woman. After this woman had experienced 12 years of loneliness and hopelessness, Jesus looked at her and called her daughter. Being a daughter is a very unique and special place in a family. She went from being all alone to being called the daughter of Jesus. How did her life change so quickly? She heard about Jesus, and she had faith that he could change her life. Jesus can change your life, too, by taking your loneliness and giving you hope in return if you are willing to simply put your faith in him.

Challenge

Reflect on each of these women from the Bible. Do you find yourself connecting with one story more than another? Why?

Talk with a friend this week and share with her the story that stood out to you. It might even help to read their stories together from the Bible.

Pray that the Jesus who encountered these women would encounter you this week in a way that would move you to have an attitude like these "old-school" ladies.

WOMEN OF THE WORLD

90 - 91

90. You Are Not Alone

In this world there are over 3 billion girls. Girls who have felt what you are feeling, who have hopes like you, and who have longed for acceptance like you. *You are not alone*, and neither are they. Imagine that somewhere in the world there is a girl just like you—the same age, the same dreams, the same fears—and while you may live in different types of homes and eat different types of foods, if you had the chance to meet, you would instantly understand each other. I know that each of us at times has felt completely alone, but that simply is not the truth. *You are not alone in this world.* Now try this: Stop and think (maybe even pray) for a girl in Addis Ababa, Ethiopia, or a girl in Pattaya, Thailand, or a girl in Tijuana, Mexico—can you imagine her? Can you begin to understand what she may be feeling right now? Now, try something a little closer to home: Pray for a girl in your town—maybe one you know or one that you don't know. Can you imagine her? Can you begin to understand what she may be feeling right now? There is power in stopping and thinking of these other girls around your town and our world because we are better when we are together. Together we are stronger. And together, we are not *alone*.

STUDENT

I have developed the habit of filling my mind with knowledge of the women in our world. I have read articles ranging from the murders of women in the Democratic Republic of the Congo to the sexual exploitation of the women we see in the tabloids at the local grocer. The sad truth is that women face oppression all over the map. To ignore the reality of the pain of our sisters everywhere is to perpetuate the problem. As women, we need each other to cope with the pain of a broken heart. Nothing is more comforting than a best friend laying her hands on you and telling you that she is there for you in prayer and that she is on your side.

By educating myself on happenings of women in the world, I have learned that although seas may separate us, we can be that best friend, that advocate who says, "I will act on your behalf and pray for you through your pain." Not only does it empower us to pray, but it compels us to move into action to fight for our sisters— to move to Thailand and bring good news to the women in brothels, to move to the victims of the war zones of Africa to heal their bodies and souls, to move to the women of the Middle East to empower and educate the women who feel shamed by their culture. Praying for those across the nations has created a secret and beautiful bond of sisterhood that is mediated by the Lord himself. It has moved me into action and has given me greater purpose for my life.

—Mackenzi, 18

91. Be a Voice

If you live in America or in another free country, then you need to appreciate what you have been given. Maybe you are unsure of exactly what you have been given. You can start with the unique rights and voice you have as a girl. Did you know that almost half of the girls in the world haven't been given the opportunity to learn to read? Or that some girls are forced to get married at the age of 12 against their will? One of the best ways to show appreciation for the gifts and rights we have been given is to speak up for those who don't have the same gifts or rights we do. Use your Facebook or MySpace page to spread the word about girls around the world. Use school papers and presentations to educate yourself and others.

Speak up for those who cannot speak for themselves; ensure justice for those being crushed. Yes, speak up for the poor and helpless, and see that they get justice (Proverbs 31:8-9).

Challenge

Reflect on the women of the world and what it means to be "sisters" with those around us and those around the world.

Talk with a friend about the injustices happening to women in the world, and share ideas about what you can do to make a difference.

Pray for the women of the world that they would hear and know Jesus and that God would use you to speak up on their behalf.

WHY BEING A
GIRL RULES

92 - 96

92. Big Hearts

You know that feeling when your heart is pounding and you can't help but feel differently than you ever have before about what you see? When God created us, he gave us big hearts—big enough to see the world and to feel the joy, pain, happiness, and sorrow all around us. When we see this in a movie or in real life, we can feel it. We are not afraid of our compassion and our willingness to feel the pain of others. We feel deeply, and these deep emotions are unique and special to girls. The next time you are overwhelmed with emotions, thank Jesus that he created you with the ability to be aware and to feel.

93. Big Hands

As deeply as we feel the needs all around us, our compassion doesn't allow us to sit still and do nothing. By our very nature we are all about action. Our compassion is matched with our action. We see a need, and we put our hands to work. Throughout history, women have been known for their ability to turn compassion into action in order to serve the needs of others. Search "famous women of history" on Google to get an idea about some of these amazing women.

94. Big Friendships

We love to laugh and experience life with others. We understand that the best moments in life are the ones shared with others. That's one of the reasons it's so easy to make fun of girls going to the bathroom together, because it's true, we prefer to be together—always. Girls tend to have a deeper understanding of relationships and our need for them. We realize that all humans want to be understood, and we tend to be more willing to allow ourselves into those big friendships even when it feels risky.

95. Big Bellies

We can have babies. I mean, when you really think about the craziness of how God created our bodies and how that within our bellies can live *another human being*, it's pretty awesome. God, in all of his creative genius, could have thought of a million different ways to create life, but he chose *us*. He placed within us our strength and our patience and our compassion. These qualities grow within you as you grow older preparing you to be a great mother. Creating life may be one of the greatest gifts and abilities that God gave to all of humankind.

96. Big Lives

Esther, Mary, Joan of Arc, Susan B. Anthony, Amelia Earhart, and Rosa Parks are just a few of history's women who lived big lives and left lasting impressions. Our lives today look the way they do because of incredible women who were available to be used by God for good, through their actions and through their voices. Being a girl doesn't mean you have to live a small life. Let women who have gone before you show you that being a girl means you can be a significant woman—you can save a generation, you can stand up against injustice, you can be an incredible mom, you can fly around the world, and you can overcome oppression—leaving this world a better place for the generations to come!

Challenge

Reflect on the unique ways in which God created girls and how being a girl changes your outlook on the world.

Talk with a friend and together create a list of things that you like about being a girl.

Pray that Jesus will fill you with more of the amazing qualities and that they will lead to life-change—through your commitment to serve at your church and around the world.

"Cautious, careful people, always casting about to preserve their reputation and social standing, never can bring about reform. Those who are really in earnest must be willing to be anything or nothing in the world's estimation."

—Susan B. Anthony, activist who campaigned for U.S. women to gain the right to vote

"Put some skates on. Be your own hero."
—Maggie Mayhem, *Whip It*

ONE MORE
THING...
97 - 99

Acknowledgements

There is no way I could have done this book without the help of my amazing husband and my cool friends. Thanks to my life group ladies, my sisters, the Ivanhearts/Swincovichs, and the Sarti Party. I am really one fortunate girl because all of you are in my life.